CONTENTIOUS CUSTODY

Is It Really in the Best Interest of Your Children?

Marlene Bizub, Psy.D.

INDIE BOOKS
INTERNATIONAL

ISBN-10: 1-941870-72-4
ISBN-13: 978-1-941870-72-3
Library of Congress Control Number: 2016955872

Designed by Joni McPherson, www.mcphersongraphics.com

INDIE BOOKS INTERNATIONAL, LLC
2424 VISTA WAY, SUITE 316
OCEANSIDE, CA 92054
www.indiebooksintl.com

CONTENTS

● ●

SECTION I

....

Why Is Child Custody a Monster Problem?

CHAPTER 1

....

The Greatest Fight of Your Life: Protecting Your Children During Divorce

> *"There is no system ever devised by mankind that is guaranteed to rip husband and wife or father, mother and child apart so bitterly than our present Family Court System."*
>
> — Judge Brian Lindsay, Retired Supreme Court Judge, New York

I n child custody cases, parents do not always have their children's best interests at heart. Parents want what they want. This leads to contentious custody battles. As a custody evaluator in Colorado for twenty years, I have witnessed the devastation when parents and professionals engage in a highly contentious process. But there is a better way.

I will never forget the day sixteen-year-old Victoria (not her real name) walked into my office. Although it had been five years since her parents' divorce, I recognized her the minute I saw her.

"I don't know if you remember me," began Victoria, "but you worked with my family several years ago. I hated you when you were working with my family."

I assured her that I was aware of those feelings on her part. We met when she as an eleven-year-old girl who had two eight-year-old twin sisters. During the divorce, Victoria had become "parentified," which is our term for a child who has to fill a parent's role. Victoria took care of the younger girls much of the time while the parents were engaging in various activities of their own.

But perhaps even more damagingly, Victoria had become a confidant to both of her parents throughout the separation and divorce process. Both parents shared adult information with Victoria, such as tales of bar-hopping escapades from her father, and news of a couple of extramarital affairs from her mother. Victoria knew all the adult issues that no child this age should know.

I finally got the parents to see how harmful this was to their child, but I did not expect for Victoria to be so adamantly opposed to not hearing all of the sundry details of her parents' new lives as single people. I brought Victoria and her parents into my office with the intent of telling Victoria that her mother and father were not going to be sharing all of the details of their lives anymore.

Victoria was not happy with me. After informing Victoria that her parents were not going to be telling her everything anymore, Victoria grabbed hold of the arms of the chair she was sitting in, leaned over the table, stared right at me, defiantly, and said, "But I need to know what's going on in my parents' lives; I *need* to know!"

I responded, "No, you don't. You need to worry about who you're going to ride bikes with when you get home; you need to be allowed to be a child."

Five years later, Victoria walked into my office and told me she'd hated me back then. But she went on to say, "I want to thank you, because you were the only person throughout my parents' divorce who allowed me to be a kid."

This is the greatest gift that we can give children in these situations. Regardless of what is going on, we need to keep them out of the middle of their parents' conflict.

Keeping the Conflict Going for Profit

The only people who profit from a divorce are attorneys. Parents are not focused on the children, but are focused on winning at all costs. Often, parents are angry at each other because of infidelity or being rejected.

The story I am about to share is not an isolated incident; in fact, it is far from it, as I have had many such incidents happen, I am disheartened to say. But this was the first and most blatant incident of this nature that had ever happened in which I was involved directly, and it was the first glimpse I had into how pervasive this problem can be in terms of the handling of these cases by the attorneys on the case.

I met with two divorcing parents (let's call them Ben and Katie) one evening in my office, the night before required mediation between the parties. The meeting had come at the request of the mother, Katie, who felt that the case could be resolved if the parents could simply talk with one another. Katie felt that it would be useful, however, for someone like myself, who was a neutral party in the case, to be present. Katie reported that the parties often got off track when talking alone with one another, and one party or the other would start bringing up past hurtful behaviors and topics that did not need to be discussed. She asserted that with the presence of a third party, the parties were more likely to stay on track with the discussion and stick to the matter at hand.

Katie started off the discussion, apologizing for placing a restraining order on the father, stating that she never really had been afraid of father. Katie stated that she knew Ben was not a danger to herself or to the children, and that she had filed the restraining order at the direction of her attorney, who had suggested that the restraining order would give mother the "upper hand" in the divorce situation, especially when it came to parenting time.

Katie went on to say that she was going to have the restraining order dropped and apologized for things she had done during the marriage that were harmful to the relationship. Ben followed suit and apologized to Katie for things that he had done during the marriage. The parties agreed on a 50/50 parenting-time plan, also agreeing on what the specific schedule for parenting time would be. The meeting ended with the parties hugging one another, and all of us were in tears. These were tears of joy for two parents who had found their way back to a relationship of peace, in the best interest of their children. Both parties expressed that they knew this was best for their children, committing to maintaining a relationship of mutual respect from that point on.

Knowing that the parties had mediation scheduled for the next day, I told Katie and Ben I would go over to the mediator's office, which was located in the courthouse, the next day to let the mediator as well as the attorneys know that the parties had worked out the issues related to parenting time.

When I arrived, the mediator was there, along with Ben. Katie and her attorney had not yet arrived. I was in the middle of explaining to the mediator that I had made his job really easy, as the parties had reached an agreement the night before, and that I was just there to tell him what the agreement was so that he could write it up in a stipulated agreement, when I heard someone walking purposefully down the hall.

I looked up to see Katie's attorney, who caught the last few words of what I was saying—primarily that the parties had reached an agreement—and the attorney said, "No, the parties *do not* have an agreement!"

Quizzically, I looked at the attorney and asked what had happened to the agreement the parties had reached the night before. The attorney replied that the father and I had bullied his client into an agreement, and that they no longer agreed (meaning Katie and her attorney, or, in actuality, her attorney; *the attorney* was the party who did not agree, if truth were known).

After asserting to the attorney that he did not know what had happened in my office the night before because he was not there, and explaining that it actually had been his client who had come up with the parenting plan on which the parents agreed, the attorney informed both the mediator and me that the parties did not have an agreement, that Katie would be seeking a supplemental evaluation, something that is permitted in the state of Colorado in family law cases, and that there was no reason to go forward with mediation that day because the parties were not going to come to any type of agreement on parenting time for their children.

Several months and many thousands of dollars later, the supplemental evaluator's report was completed, recommending the same parenting time as my evaluation had recommended, and the same parenting-time plan that the parties had agreed to that night in my office. Katie and Ben, as well as their children, had to go through another evaluation; the parties' and their children's lives were put on hold that much longer, precluding their ability to get on with life following the break-up of the parents; and the parties were much poorer following this unnecessary and, in my mind, unethical delay in finding closure to the new family scenario.

I told this story to another attorney after all was said and done. This attorney, who knew the mother's attorney on a personal basis, told me that mother's attorney had "failed to plan very well for retirement," as she put it, indicating to me that the attorney intentionally kept cases going and perpetuated conflict between the parties in order to do so, in order to earn more money at a time when the attorney was approaching retirement and was ill-prepared for it.

I would love to be able to say, as mentioned previously, that this was an isolated incident, and that this type of thing does not happen very often in the family law arena. But the truth of the matter is that it happens all the time; *all the time*.

Another similar story involves a mother who decided to leave a marriage that was abusive, but in order to get out of the marriage, she was going to have to leave the children with father for a period of time while she got on her feet. When the mother left the family home, the father involved the older child, who was only four years old at the time, by saying things like, "Tell your whore mother goodbye. Say 'goodbye, whore mommy' to your mother," which the child tearfully repeated. Father then said, "Tell her to have fun sleeping for her supper," which the child again tearfully repeated. Father, of course, meant to imply that mother would have to sleep around in order to have food and shelter for herself. Although the child did not know at age four what these things meant, he knew enough to know that things were bad between the parents and mommy was leaving, not knowing if or when she would return. The father continued with a few other such statements, which are too graphic to share here, but which the child dutifully repeated, as his father told him to do.

The amazing thing about this story, however, is that several years later, when the mother now had the children a significant amount of the time, mother was heard encouraging the child to enjoy his time with daddy, even when the child did not want to go. Mother stated, "But daddy wants to spend time with you, too. He loves you too, you know. You'll have a good time." When I asked mother how she could rise above the things that had been done to her and encourage time spent with father, the mother stated, "It's still his father, and it does no good for me to put him down. That only hurts my son and makes him feel badly about himself." This mother got it!

Regardless of what her ex had said or done to her, this was a mother who recognized that the child needs his father and needs to feel positively about his father, and the mother was able to facilitate the sharing of love and affection between the child and his father.

And it didn't end there for this mother. As she encouraged the child to enjoy the time he was going to spend with his now-stepmother, I could not help but ask how she was able to uphold her in the middle of all of this, as the father had certainly not behaved the same when it came to the child spending time with his stepfather, whom the father had told the child was the reason the parents did not get back together, because mother had "chosen stepfather over keeping the family together." Mother stated, "He can't have enough adults in his life who love him," speaking of the child benefitting from having loving adults in his life. In this instance, mother was able to love her child more than she disliked the actions of his father, and this is something that many parents are unable to do.

It is important to understand the needs of our children through the divorce and custody resolution process, and their needs will vary from stage to stage in the developmental progression through childhood and adolescence. The following Developmental Stage Chart helps to identify the needs of the children at different ages in the context of their parents' divorce or separation:

The Developmental Stages and Needs of Children

••

When parents are divorcing, here are some guiding principles to consider:

- No matter how much pain you are going through yourself, minimize the child/ren's sense of loss.

- Make small changes.

- Make changes gradually.

- Remember that children have not yet developed complete logic. They make conclusions from incomplete information.

- Remember that children are egocentric. They unconsciously believe they cause life's difficulties.

- Remember, also, that you and your children are individuals. What works for other families may not work for you and your family.

Age Range	Developmental Tasks	Needs	Helpful Parental Behavior
Birth to 2.5 years	Trust and bonding Self-awareness	Love and affection, predictability and consistency	Frequent, regular contact with both parents Follow similar routines Protect baby's "personal environment" Never criticize other parent in front of child Communicate with one another Attend to and respond to baby's cues
Preschool 2.5 to 5 years	Independence Gender identification Sense of identity Language and concept development	Love and affection, predictability and consistency Routines and structure Limits and consequences Freedom to explore safely Playing with other children Intellectual and physical stimulation	Same as for birth to 2.5 Establish family rules as consistently as possible Discuss child's feelings with him or her Check with other caregivers without biasing them to discover child's adjustment
Early elementary 5-8 years	Developing friendships Mastering school skills, social skills, and physical skills	Same as 2.5 to 5 Parent-school interaction Extrafamilial activities Opportunities for success in school, home and extra activities	Same as 2.5 to 5 Keep children out of communication loop Keep open lines of communication between parents, school, sports, and other group leaders Both parents attend child's events Encouraging friendships
Late elementary 9-12 years	Learn logical and problem-solving Develop peer relationships Athletics and other interests gain importance	Continue from above Greater peer contact Guidance in problem-solving Extracurricular activities to discover interests	Same as above Continued communication with others who are involved in child's life Establish activities for personal enrichment with child's input; however, do not over-plan the child's life Encourage continued social development Allow some privacy
Adolescence	Individuation and separation Gender identification Sexual maturation, understanding & awareness Work ethic	Loyal friendships Opportunities to be successful in school, craft, sport, work, etc. Development of social skills in peer interaction & dating relationships	Same as above Less rigid parenting schedules to accommodate friendships & activities Allow child to have greater input into parenting-time plan

(Reproduced with permission from Janet Jones, MA, LPC)

The thing that is important to remember is that all children are different, not only in their ages and levels of maturity, but in regard to such things as resilience, temperament, and other aspects of their personalities, as well as individual traits and characteristics that affect their responses to their parents' divorce or separation. Taking the individual needs of a child into consideration is a must in helping them to cope effectively with the change in their family structure.

SECTION II

Identifying the Monster

CHAPTER 2

······································

The Monster's Lair—Family Court

"Our first advice for divorcing families is to stay as far away from matrimonial attorneys and family court judges as possible."

— Families Civil Liberties Union (http://www.fclu.org/)

The family court is a civil war. "The more exposure to the family court system, the less your family will end up with, and the more adversarial your relationship will be," says the Families Civil Liberties Union. "The family court acts as the front-end sales and marketing arm for lawyers, 'experts,' and a host of other unnecessary service providers, including the jail system, and orders their costly use to victims on a daily basis. Family court is quite literally American Bar Association (ABA)-controlled, state-sanctioned job creation, racketeering, fraud, and theft of family assets. The

ABA fights tooth-and-nail to block any reform in the interest of defrauding innocent families."

It is an unhealthy, caustic environment where people become all about "winning" and, for at least the time being, set their values aside in order to "score a win." The system is set up this way to create winners and losers. In a long-distance case, for example, in which parents live in separate geographical locations, the Court is not going to be able to please both parents, as there is no "splitting the baby," so to speak. Both parents typically want to have the children during the academic school year, with the other parent having the summer with the children. There is no way to create an equitable parenting-time plan for parents in this situation. Even for parents who live in the same city, often one parent will believe that the children need to be in the same home during the school week and in the other home on the weekend, while the other parent sees no harm in splitting up both the school week and the weekend. Or perhaps both parents agree that the children should be in one home during the week, but both parents believe that that home should be his or her home. Again, in any of these scenarios, both parents are not going to be able to have their way. Parents have incompatible desires, creating a "win/lose" situation.

Although the role of an attorney is to advocate for his or her client to the best of his or her ability, attorneys are also the ones who understand the system and how the system works. This holds true for other professionals who work within the system as well, such as evaluators and mediators. The clients (divorcing or separating parents) only know what those working within the system teach them. There are clients who will want an attorney to engage in unethical conduct, and it is up to those who have integrity and an ethical social barometer to say, "no, we are not engaging in that type of behavior or action."

The parents are operating with raw emotion at this time in their lives, and many will behave in ways that they have never behaved before and will perhaps never behave again. They are perhaps angry right now and are trying to make decisions that they will have to live with, perhaps for a long time, when they are really not in an emotional place to do so. Professionals involved can either pit them against one another, which is often the tendency of the parents, or bring them back to their senses by using logic, rather than emotion, to make the decisions that truly are best for their children.

Parents often pressure their attorneys to make sure the parent "wins," but a parent in the middle of divorce or separation cannot always see what it really means to "win," or what it is that is really a "win" for the children. In other words, a parent "winning" by getting what he or she wants is not always a "win" for the children. As long as parents stay focused on beating the other parent rather than on their children, the outcome will be parent-oriented, not child-oriented. All parties must work together, both parents and attorneys alike, to look for an outcome that serves the best interest of the children, not one that is designed to get back at the other parent. And sometimes, getting back at the other parent is actually detrimental to the children, who often learn things about the other parent that they really did not need to know—at least not at this stage in their lives.

Often, for example, attorneys will direct me to the Facebook page of the "other" parent in the case (the party who the attorney is not representing). Perhaps the person has left something on their page showing behavior not very becoming of the parent, or perhaps a rant venting at the time the other parent sprung on them, sometimes from out of nowhere, that they wished to leave the marriage. Parties often post these kinds of things on social media because they assume that the children are not going to be looking there, or it's the only venue they have to vent without calling all of their friends and bending their ears, knowing that friends don't want to hear all their problems or don't want to feel as though they have been placed in the middle of the fight between the two parents. People often trust that social media is a "safe" place to express what they are feeling, and divorcing parents often do this when feelings are still raw.

Children, however, often *do* access these pages, as they have grown up on social media. Children, especially teenagers, often have their own Facebook pages. Parents are leaving the door open for their children to access information that the children simply do not need to hear. Even if the children do not access these rants or the posts intended only for adult eyes, what parent wants to have all of the details of their lives plastered on the pages of social media for all of the world to know and see?

Similarly, attorneys also often run background checks on the other parent and bring up things that happened long before the children had arrived or were even a thought in the parent's mind: a DUI that happened when a parent was still young and making unwise choices but that the parent thought they had sufficiently concealed from the rest of the world becomes public knowledge when the other parent decides to post the newfound revelation on their own social media page. And once it is "out there," it is often impossible to retract or re-conceal.

During this time, the worst seems to come out in people as they seek to destroy the other parent; sometimes intentionally, sometimes not, but they do exactly that when they fail to think through the implications of their actions.

I have seen parents cause other parents to lose their jobs with the information they reveal, never thinking that if the other parent is unemployed, it will be awfully difficult for them to pay child support or maintenance should child support or maintenance be awarded. Likewise, I have seen parents have the other party arrested for violating a restraining order (sometimes one that was ill-placed to begin with) failing to consider that if the other parent is in jail, they may lose their employment. I have seen parents in military families lose security clearances, which affects their places within the organization, or causes them to lose their jobs altogether, especially if they are, for example, military contractors and filling positions that require security clearance.

Again, it is often difficult to determine whether it is the attorney who is driving the hostility or whether it is a parent wishing to get back at their soon-to-be-ex, who has perhaps betrayed or rejected them. Especially in a state that is a "no-fault" divorce state, digging up all the dirt one parent can against the other has little impact on the outcome of a custody determination.

However, parents seem to have a tendency to do just that, perhaps out of vengefulness, or because of the hurt and pain that go along with the end of a relationship that they thought would last forever.

Additionally, this desire to destroy the other parent, regardless of who is prompting the actions, often destroys other relationships within the family. Parents who enlist the involvement of other family members in their campaign against the other parent often damages relationships among family members beyond repair, as well as destroying their own relationships with these family members. This becomes especially harmful when it involves the participation of the children. In the short-term, the parent often turns the child against the other parent. Rarely, however, does this last. The child often starts feeling a sense of guilt and shame for their role in the destruction of the parent and this, in turn, often causes the child to resent the parent who enlisted their involvement in the first place.

In one of the worst cases of this nature that I witnessed in my career as an evaluator, a daughter was used to obtain information about the mother that the father believed he could use against mother in court. Father solicited the teenage daughter's assistance in making copies of checks that mother had written and sending them to father. The daughter did so, but later started feeling guilty for her actions, as she knew the behavior was wrong. Eventually, the daughter confessed her involvement to mother and asked for her mother's forgiveness. But the father's involvement of the daughter had damaged their relationship beyond repair. The daughter was angry and resentful of father for involving her in this manner, and those feelings had a lasting effect. In cases such as this, the relationship the parent eventually destroys is his or her own parent-child relationship.

CHAPTER 3

··

Let's You and You Fight: When Attorneys Extend the Battle

Whatever the impetus that causes the attorneys or other professionals within the family court system to behave the way they do, it is something that is difficult to deal with and creates a "battleground" environment. The players within this system are embroiled in a conflict that is sometimes so intense that people actually battle when it comes to parenting time, or what is still called "visitation" in many states. Because what greater battle is there than the fight over one's children?

This is, however, the worst possible time for parents to be making decisions about their children. Parents may be (and generally are) very angry at this time, and decisions made out of anger are rarely the best decisions. It is often said within the family court system that the participants—the divorcing parents—are generally good people who are at a bad time in their lives.

Whereas in criminal court, we typically see bad people who, for that period of time, are on their best behavior, the opposite is true for the parties in a domestic relations case. The parents are often on their worst behavior, engaging in behaviors that they typically would not exhibit. It is like the difference, often seen in these cases, between parties engaging in "pushy-shovey" behavior and parties who are true batterers. Parties become emotionally charged and, in the heat of anger, may push one another, as opposed to a true batterer who beats the other party. In these cases, often feelings do not manifest themselves in physical actions, but rather emotional. The things parties say to one another in the middle of a break-up are often not things the parties have ever said before or will ever say again. This behavior is the product of people being at the worst time of their lives, going through the worst experience of their lives, but also momentarily forgetting the people who are most important in this situation—the children.

Some parents have the ability to place the needs of their children above their own in this situation, and some don't. Or another way of putting it: some parents love their children more than they hate their soon-to-be ex-spouse or significant other. This is really what it boils down to; can each individual place the needs of the children above whatever anger they have toward the other parent, and their former "soul mate"?

It is perhaps the death of that dream—that this is the person who will be my best friend for the rest of my life and we will all live happily ever after—that stings the worst. It makes us wonder if such an idealistic relationship exists out there, or are all relationships doomed to fail once we really get to know each other and find out what each other is truly like to live with, day in and day out? It challenges the most basic belief that we are taught from a very young age: that we are going to meet the man or woman of our dreams, fall in love, and live happily ever after. Then we find out that rarely does this happen. We all know that the divorce rate is around the 50 percent mark for first-time marriages, and even higher for subsequent marriages.

And even that does not tell the whole story. There are many people who are still in an intact family, where mommy and daddy have stayed together, but the marriage is not a happy one, with a lot of arguing and conflict that takes place within the relationship—hardly the "happily ever after" vision that they had when they said "I do." But this figure is just for marriages. It does not take into account the higher percentage of break-ups that occur in relationships that never make it to the altar, but produced children nonetheless. It is difficult to track statistics for such relationships, but I read an article the other day[1] which indicated that for

[1] http://www.slate.com/articles/business/moneybox/2014/06/for_millennials_out_of_wedlock_childbirth_is_the_norm_now_what.html

millennials, out-of-wedlock childbirth is the norm. So there is a statistic indicating how many relationships that produce children and end in separation that is certain to be *higher* than the 50 percent statistic we see for committed relationships in which parties have publicly said, "I do."

Let's face it; no one teaches us how to have a successful break-up. This is not the ideal, so why would we prepare people for it? Relationships, especially ones that make it all the way to the altar, are not supposed to end this way, or are not supposed to *end*. At all. Period. So no one talks about how to make it better when it happens, the 50 percent of the time that it does with marriages, and the higher unknown percentage for the relationships that produce children but never make it to "married" status. Often, the example that has been set by family members who have gone through the break-up of a child-producing relationship is not a good one. Conflict and fighting are expected. People talk with great pride about relationships that continue peacefully, because they really do not "end," primarily because it is not expected and is somewhat of an anomaly. We are seeing more of it, thankfully, but it is still not anywhere near the norm for separating couples.

It has become my belief, from years of working in the area of family law, that a big part of the reason this remains such an anomaly is because separations are handled within a system that perpetuates the conflict. There is something to be gained by continuing the conflict—by encouraging discord and perpetuating relationships in which people are at odds with one another; in which they are *enemies*. This type of relationship is encouraged, even though it is often played out in the presence of our children, furthering an environment of conflict and passing this way of handling a break-up on to the next generation rather than setting a better example of a healthier, more productive way to manage the end of a relationship.

As much as I hate to say that there is financial gain in perpetuating the conflict, it is the truth. Divorce attorneys and others who work within the family law system capitalize on conflict. There is something to be gained by the ongoing discord, and that is the financial gain of professionals working within this framework. And the more issues of contention, the greater the financial gain. For each issue the parties argue about, the cost of divorce becomes higher and higher.

In a recent case in which I was the evaluator (ironically one in which the client went on a vicious campaign of attack against me) the client called in to a local consumer advocate radio program complaining that his divorce had cost him $80,000 to date, and the parties were not divorced yet. For each issue of contention, each item of disagreement, the bill for representation in order to "settle" those issues grew higher and higher.

As with Katie and Ben from Chapter 1, this was another parent who was unhappy with the recommendations I had made and asked for a supplemental evaluation. Again, the supplemental evaluation was granted, and again the recommendations came back nearly identical to the ones that I had made in the first evaluation.

The harm that is done in these situations is to the children in these cases, who often have to endure unnecessary and repeated evaluations. The children have to relive their parents' break-up, and the details of the arguments and other specifics that led to the parents' separation. It also delays the children's ability to process what has happened, grieve the loss of their family as they knew it, and move on.

If adults wish to continue fighting, that is one thing. But the unnecessary, unacceptable involvement of the children in the fight is just unconscionable! The emotional harm to the children far outweighs any benefit or gain there is to the parents, and actually there is no gain or benefit to the parents. In the case of Ben and Katie, described in Chapter 1, Katie did not do herself any good; she gained no benefit in the divorce situation, and if anything, ended up looking wishy-washy, at best, for handling the situation the way she did, for allowing her attorney to handle it the way he did.

As a separating or divorcing parent, it is important to insulate yourself from being manipulated or pressured into unproductive, excessive, and potentially destructive conflicts rather than moving on to resolutions that will be the most beneficial to not only you as the parents, but also that will preserve your children's emotional health and well-being, as well. As tempting as it may be to take a destructive approach, especially if you are angry and bitter toward your soon-to-be ex-spouse or partner right now, rarely does this approach bode well in court. But how do you gauge whether or not your attorney's approach is excessive or in your best interest?

For starters, listen to your inner voice, which usually is not wrong. Weigh whether you believe in what the attorney is suggesting, or whether it just feels good right now. One suggestion is to ask yourself how you would respond if a friend of yours told you that they were going to approach his or her divorce in this manner. Or ask trusted family members or friends, with an emphasis on *trusted*, what they think about what your attorney is suggesting. Make sure they are people with good judgment, not those who will simply go along with whatever you suggest, or whatever your attorney suggests. Solicit those who you know do not relish gaining revenge, but will take a more balanced and unbiased view.

It is also a good idea to have some awareness of how you resolve conflict. Using a tool such as a conflict-style questionnaire (available online or through professional counselors and therapists) will help to assess your style of resolving conflict, as well as the other parent's style. Then the two of you can compare your styles of conflict resolution and identify impediments to your ability to resolve conflicts together, in light of the manner by which both of you resolve conflicts.

Once you each understand your style of conflict resolution, the other parent's style of conflict resolution, and how those two styles impact one another, it will be easier to address conflicts from a more enlightened perspective and potentially head off barriers to the two of you resolving conflicts appropriately and effectively. Even though you are no longer a couple, as coparents to your children you will continue to have conflicts that must be resolved for as long as you are raising your children, and perhaps even longer. Understanding how to do that effectively will save everyone a lot of turmoil, reduce the tension, and alleviate the stress between the two of you.

In addition, you can also utilize your newfound understanding of how you tend to handle conflicts and confrontation in interactions you have with others as well. You can, for example, use this awareness to arm yourself in discussions with your divorce attorney to ensure that you do not allow yourself as a parent to be manipulated or pressured into unproductive or destructive communications with your former mate. Rather, insist on eliciting conversations aimed toward identifying resolutions that will be the most beneficial to your children.

CHAPTER 4

....

What's "Winning" When It Comes to Custody?

So what is it that causes the parties in custody cases to allow themselves to be represented in the manner that we often see in family court cases? The parties, at this particular time in their lives, are vulnerable. They are often fragile, emotionally and otherwise, and are not making the best decisions that they could be making. Often they do not know what decisions they should be making and have to rely on the attorney they've selected to help navigate through the decisions that have to be made. The parties do not know what is typical, or what is expected of them, in these situations.

Attorneys will often convince parents that the court expects them to fight over their children, as though this is somehow going to be perceived as a good thing. Or, worse yet, the attorney will convince the parent that they can get a "better deal" in the parenting-time situation. Often, attorneys have made their clients promises and now they have to find a way to fulfill that promise, which often was an ill-made promise in the first place. Or if the attorney stopped short of making a promise, he or she perhaps at least alluded to an expected outcome, saying that this is the way it usually turns out, creating an expected outcome on the part of the parent.

Parents who are separating often do not know what is typical or is expected in these cases. They rely on attorneys, who often do not have the client's best interest at heart. Worse yet, the parent listens too much to people around them who think that it's best if one parents "wins custody" of the children. The concept of shared parenting, and especially peaceful shared parenting, is something that has only really come into existence within the last generation. Even in my parents' divorce, one of my parents had "custody" and the other had "visitation" (terms that have thankfully been omitted from Colorado, where I have conducted the work that I have for the courts, and other states' statutes). Parents also often do not know or understand the terms, such as "primary custody." I always have to clarify their intent with parents when they come into my office and say, "I want to be the primary parent." I have to ask what they mean by that: do they want the majority of the parenting time with the children? Do they want to have sole decision-making for the children? What exactly do they mean when they say that they wish to be the "primary parent"? Or when they say they want "sole custody," do they mean that they do not want the other parent to see the children? Or if they do want the other parent to see them, how much do they want the other parent to see the children?

Often the parents themselves do not know the answers to these questions, or what they mean when they come in using certain terms. It's simply a term they have heard from someone else, and they have decided that this is what they want in this scenario. Sometimes parents will say to me, "I just want the standard every-other-weekend schedule" (meaning for the *other* parent, of course). But parents say this not realizing that the courts, at least in Colorado, have not had a "standard" schedule of every-other-weekend parenting time for one of the parents for many years, at least for as long as I have been doing this type of work, which is about twenty years. Rarely does a parent wanting "sole custody" envision that the other parent will not see the children at all. But the amount of time that they envision the other parent will have the children varies widely from person to person. Some parents envision that the other parent will have every other weekend with the children; some envision that it will be close to 50/50, but that they will at least have one more day per year than the other parent, thus making them the "primary parent." Yes, some truly want only whatever it takes to deem them the "primary parent" in the eyes of the court, or the world. "Primary parent" becomes a status symbol for this type of person.

I would love to say that the following is a rare conversation that I have in my office, but it is not. One parent comes in, and we discuss what the parent thinks would be a good parenting-time schedule for their children. And this parent says, "Well, I thought for each of us to have every other week would be good for the children, but my attorney told me I could get a much better deal, given that my ex likes to drink," (or works late hours, or whatever other deficit the parent can find in the other parent). I especially react to the term "better deal" when it comes to parenting-time schedules. Some parents really view it this way, perhaps perpetuated by their attorney, perhaps viewing it this way independently. But to this parent, the parenting-time schedule boils down to how good a "deal" the parent can get in the parenting-time negotiations. If the view is perpetuated by the attorney, I often wonder how this conversation took place in the office of the attorney, and am curious what the reaction of the parent was the first time they heard, "I can get you a better deal than that."

I have an idea of how that conversation goes, as only recently I heard an attorney make such a comment in my office. The two parents, their respective attorneys, and I met in my office for a "5-way" meeting, to discuss parenting time and see if we could reach an agreement. This was another scenario in which I had met with the parents the night before in my office, and we had hammered out a parenting-time plan. The parents and I had reached an agreement that we thought was best for the child in the case. The following day at the 5-way, one of the attorneys said in the middle of a discussion about the parenting-time schedule, "I'm not sure this is best for my client," and asked to have a few minutes alone with his client before proceeding with the meeting. My thought, although I did not say it out loud, was, "This is not about what is best for your client; it is about what is best for the *child*." Although I understand, as stated previously, that the job of an attorney is to advocate for their client, is there not a point at which we all make it our primary focus to do what is in the best interest of the child? (I am afraid I know the answer to this question!)

Further perpetuating the conflict in these cases is the interrelationship between parenting time and how much child support is going to be paid by one parent or received by the other. If I had one wish in the parenting-time situation, it would be that child support was not based on the amount of parenting time that a parent has or, more specifically, the number of overnights that each parent has. It is truly my belief that we would quickly find out what a parent genuinely wants in the way of parenting time if there were not a dollar amount attached to it, either in what one parent is going to pay or in what the other parent is going to receive. If child support was not based on the number of overnights that each parent has with the children, we would not have this problem. There is a formula that also takes into consideration the amount of income that each parent earns, even allowing for imputed income for parents who do not work or who are voluntarily unemployed or underemployed. But it is all still tied to the number of overnights each parent has with the children. I sincerely believe that parents would view the schedule differently if this association between overnights and parenting time did not exist.

One recent example of this that I had in a case involved a 5-year-old girl who does not do well away from the primary caregiver, who in this case happened to be the mother, and also involved a mother and stepmother who did not get along. In fact, one of the recommendations I had made in this case was for the parents to exchange the child with one another by themselves and, specifically, for the stepmother to refrain from being present during the exchange of the child from one parent to the other, as stepmother was creating conflict and chaos between the parties during the exchanges. When it came down to figuring out the parenting-time schedule, father had a work schedule in which he got up at 5:00 in the morning in order to be at work at 6:00 a.m. on Saturdays. Father wanted to keep the child overnight on Friday, even though it would necessitate mother doing the exchange of the child with the stepmother on Saturday morning. Mother proposed picking the child up on Friday evening, even offering to wait until bedtime to pick the child up, and asserted that father would not be spending time with the child on Saturday morning anyway, as father would already be at work when the child awakened.

Due to the fact that parenting time is based on the number of overnights each parent has, father was not willing to forego this overnight with the child. Father had agreed that it should be the parents, and not the stepmother, conducting the exchange of the child. But when it came down to father having one less overnight with the child, father was unwilling to do so, opting instead to force the two women to have contact with one another, even though this often did not go well, and whatever conflict occurred between them was usually played out in the presence of the child, who was obviously present for the exchange. Father was losing nothing but sleeping time with the child, as father was gone in the morning long before the child was awake. Mother offered to do the transporting of the child herself, and to wait until bedtime to pick the child up, therefore ensuring that father still had all of the waking time with the child that he possibly could have. Since Friday was not a school night, mother was not worried about the child getting to bed a little later than usual in order to allow father to have as much time as possible with the child that evening. But father refused to allow mother to pick the child up on Friday evening.

Knowing this father as I did, after working with the parties for an extended period of time during the evaluation process, I am convinced that if it did not make a difference in the amount of child support father paid, he would not have minded one bit if mother picked the child up on Friday night. In fact, father often had mother pick the child up early during his parenting time because, for one reason or another, father could not keep the child.

This raises another often-seen practice of some parents; to request having the child (and write it into their parenting-time plan) at a time when the parent is simply not available to parent the child. This is another practice that is born out of the association between child support and overnights. This association contributes to, if not outright causes, parents having the children during times that the parent is not going to be available. This makes no logical sense, but it does affect the amount of child support paid. Therefore, it is not uncommon to see parenting-time schedules that routinely have one parent scheduled with the child at a time when the parent is not available. This often results in the parent scrambling to find someone to watch the child, or simply relying on the other parent to have the child. Most caring parents are willing to help bail out the other parent by taking the child in a situation such as this, but it costs them in the amount of child support they receive, simply because the other parent does not want to pay a penny more than they can get away with paying. This is irrespective of the fact that the parent who is being relied on is the one having to pay for the child's expenses at the time. Rarely does a parent in this situation provide food or other necessities for the other parent, who is being kind enough to keep the child on the other parent's time. And for families with four or five children, this can add up to a significant amount in the way of expenses.

It is my belief that most people would not even realize such things as the relationship between overnights and child support if it had not been brought up by an attorney in the case. Most parents do not realize until after parenting time has been decided how much they are going to pay in child support and how the number of overnights is going to affect the child support amount. When parents come into my office counting the number of overnights they are going to have, I am fairly certain that someone has been talking with them about the relationship between the number of overnights and the amount of child support they are going to pay or receive. In the state of Colorado, there is a number at which the parties move from *Worksheet A* to *Worksheet B* in calculating child support, and there are benefits each way to keeping the number of overnights below that number, or getting the number of overnights above that number. This also affects the parenting time that each parent desires, and sometimes parents openly say, "I have to keep it above ninety-two overnights per year" (or whatever the magic number is that moves the calculation from *Worksheet A* to *Worksheet B*).

It is hard to believe that parents truly decide what they want in the way of a parenting-time schedule based on things such as this, and I probably would not have believed how pervasive it was had I not witnessed it myself every time a parent came into my office seeking whatever it was that they were seeking, based on the effect it was going to have on the child support amount. How awful would the children feel if they knew they were desired by a parent for this reason. And the sad thing is, many of them do. It is usually the older children, but on more than one occasion I've had children tell me that if one of the parents can have a certain amount of time with the children, it will affect the amount of child support they receive or pay, and in turn that affects something having to do with the child, such as getting a car. I had one child tell me exactly this—that if dad did not have to pay mom as much child support as she wanted, dad could buy the child a car. Dad actually told the child this! Therefore, I had a teenager telling me that he wanted more time with his father, and had already told me that this was the reason why. It did not seem to bother the teenager, of course, as he was a typical teenager and was focused on getting what he wanted (in this case, a car). One can see, however, the predicament this kind of situation puts an evaluator in; we have to decide how to handle parenting time recommendations knowing this is the underlying factor involved.

CHAPTER 5

••

Where Does the Monster Live? Identifying the Source of the Problem—Parent or Attorney

I n order to identify solutions to the problems within the family court system, one must identify the source of the problem, and that is not always easy to do. There are factors that perpetuate the problems, however, and these may be easy to see when one steps back and looks at the family court system. But it is not so easy to see when you are a parent in the middle of a contentious divorce or separation. And it is not so easy to know what to do about these problems if and when a parent starts to recognize them.

For one thing, a parent is often already far into the process of obtaining their divorce when they realize that they have an attorney whose style is to fight every step of the way and perpetuate the conflict. Often, a parent is faced with the dilemma of whether it is cheaper to stay with this attorney, who knows the case intimately even if he or she is in "fight mode," or start over with an attorney who does not know anything about the case. And what if the next attorney ends up being as contentious as the previous attorney? Although there are websites one can access that offer ratings for different attorneys, they are not always reliable, as people tend to post things on such sites based more on their happiness with the outcome of the case rather than basing their opinions on the performance or conduct of the attorney.

It is not always the attorney who wishes to fight, however. It is often the parent who wishes to keep the battle going. It has often been difficult for me, as an evaluator, to ascertain exactly which party it is—the parent or the attorney—who is perpetuating the conflict. There is a tendency for some attorneys to take on the personality or posture of the parent who is the client in the case. In some cases, it appears that the attorney wishes to keep the conflict going, and in some cases it appears to be the parent who is determined to "win" and destroy the other parent in the process. It seems that too often parents get caught up with an overzealous attorney who is going to get them a "better deal," causing an otherwise well-intentioned parent to make decisions or behave in a manner that he or she would not have engaged in before.

Sadly, I recently heard a local attorney tell the audience during a court-ordered coparenting class that often the first question she is asked by clients calling to elicit her services is, "What is your 'win/ loss' ratio?" How does one determine, in a family law case, what is a "win" and what is a "loss"? Is it determined by how pleased the client is at the end of the case? And if the client is more pleased than displeased, it that a "win"?

The fact remains that in nearly every case (at least the ones in which I have been involved), one party is relatively pleased and one is relatively displeased. And often it is the case that neither parent is pleased with the outcome. Sometimes what each parent wants is so far away from what the other wants that there is no way either party is ever going to be pleased with the outcome unless as an evaluator I clearly agree with one of the sides; rarely is that the case. More times than not, what happens is that what is best for the children is something smack dab in the middle of what the two parents want, so there is no way either parent, on opposite ends of a spectrum, is going to be happy.

I also often hear from parents that they are seeking a "bulldog" of an attorney for their case and they ask if I can make a referral. My first question is, do you want a "bulldog," or do you want someone who presents well to the court and is respected by the judges in these cases? Believe it or not, I sometimes hear that they want the bulldog! And this is what they seek, never realizing that a "bulldog" may not serve their best interests well and may not be able to obtain the result that they desire. Yet some believe that this is what they want or need in order to get what they desire. If this is the case, I do not know how that can be best for the children, because it certainly does not promote an air of civility in the case.

I get no greater joy in these cases than when I am able to tell the children who I have been serving that their parents worked out an agreement amicably and that there will be no need to go to court because the parents decided, on their own and together, what they thought would be best for the children. And that is exactly what the family gets in a scenario such as this. Because what is truly best for the children is for the *parents* to decide what is best for their children. Who better knows the needs of the children than the parents? It certainly is not a judge, who may hear two or three hours' worth of information about the family before making a decision as important and full of impact than what the parenting time schedule will be. And only half of that time is being spent on parenting time issues. The other half is spent on financial and property matters (the other considerations in a divorce case).

What parents often do not realize is that the most devastating part of parents separating or divorcing for the children is conflict between the parents. Whatever the issues are that the parents are fighting about, whether it is the exchange location for transferring the children from one parent's care to the other, or what time the parent has the child for a particular holiday, or any of the other issues that separating parents typically fight about, it is the conflict itself that poses the greatest potential of harm or difficulty for the child. Some parents fight about every little issue or detail in regard to the parenting-time plan, and often fight about things that that have little real impact on the parenting plan. Many parents fight just for the sake of fighting, or for the sake of "winning." Or many times it is just for the sake of maintaining some level of control over the other parent.

If you are a separating or divorcing parent, choose your battles wisely. Before you argue about every little thing, just bear in mind that it is conflict between parents, moreso than whatever it is that you're fighting about, that poses the greatest risk of harm to your children.

SECTION III

···

Slaying the Monster Together: A Mutually Agreed-Upon Plan

CHAPTER 6

···

Negotiation Basics for Divorcing Parents: A Crash Course

Once parents realize the damage that is done by exposing their children to conflict, how do two separating or divorcing parents arrive at an agreement about what is best for their children? The parents are perhaps coming off of months, if not years, of arguing about everything under the sun because the marriage, in the true sense of the word, has been over for years and the parents have merely been tolerating one another, in the "best interest of the children."

Rarely is this really best, as the parties tend to bicker, and children can tell when their parents are unhappy with one another. Children can often see the divorce coming before the parents even do. More times than not, unfortunately, the parents are not going to reach an agreement by "lawyering up" and going into battle, especially if they select contentious attorneys who wish to perpetuate the fight. And, as already discussed, having a judge make the decision is not best, as they will hear and know very little about the family at the time they make the decision.

Most states now require that parties go to mediation prior to holding a contested hearing in the case. This is a great idea in theory; most mediators, however, fall into the same category as the judge. The mediator will know very little about the family. The mediator will try to broker a deal with the parents based on even less information that the judge will have, as mediators usually know nothing, or very little, about the family at the time mediation takes place. Too often, mediation is merely another item to check off the list before the parties enter into battle in the courtroom to determine what is in the best interest of their children.

The concept of negotiating an agreement is a wonderful idea, as long as the person doing the negotiating between the parents can spend a little bit more time getting to know the details of the family and the needs of the children.

Parents often do not know what the court is likely to do in a situation like theirs, and a lot of bad information can come from friends or coworkers who had an unusual outcome or who think that they know what a court is likely to do in a case such as theirs. Every case is different, and the specifics of the case have everything to do with the outcome, but most parents do not know what factors matter and what things weigh more heavily than others.

There is also the age-old problem of lack of consistency in these cases. Each judge may handle things differently, as long as they remain within the confines of the statute, which is often poorly written or leaves too much open to interpretation.

In the state of Colorado, there is the "Best Interest of the Child" statute, which lists the factors that are taken into consideration by the court when determining parenting-time cases. Different judges emphasize or place more weight on certain items over others. Many states, including Colorado, have either considered or passed a presumption in favor of a 50/50 parenting-time plan. Although Colorado has not passed such a statute yet, it is always up for discussion when it comes time to review the statutes that govern parenting-time litigation.

Professionals cannot know in a matter of two or three hours what things are major concessions to a parent, because the parent has probably never thought about it in these terms before. The parties, however, do not need to go to the other end of the spectrum and engage in battle by hiring a highly contentious, not to mention expensive, attorney to get them what they want. It usually does not happen that way, and the parent is only further dismayed by the process in the end.

Parents have to realize that they cannot buy an outcome, and when they start thinking that this is what they are doing, this is where the trouble begins. The important concept for a parent to keep in mind is that outcomes cannot be purchased at any price. And sometimes the more contentious attorneys who are putting on a show in the courtroom, usually for the benefit of the parent who hired them, are not well received by judged, and the outcome is not at all what the parent expected.

Perhaps the best option for separating or divorcing parents is to use a neutral third person who can spend a little more time getting to know the family, including the children, and can assist the family in negotiating the matters that arise when parties separate. One concept that parents often forget is that they are not going to win every disagreement.

In working with separating parents, I use a negotiation process that emphasizes the fact that they will not get everything they want. Therefore, parties are asked to list the things that matter to them, placing them in three different categories.

- **One:** Things that the parent does not really care a lot about at all

- **Two:** Things that are up for negotiation

- **Three:** Things upon which that parent stands firm, because he or she feels very strongly about this issue and is not open to much negotiation about this particular issue at all

The overriding principle in this process is for parents to not place themselves in a position in which they feel they have to make a major concession, all the while realizing that they will not get everything they want. The important part, though, is not to feel as though they had to make a major concession, because then they will have trouble with "buy-in" to the agreement.

This concept of not ever having to make a major concession is the most important aspect parents need to keep in mind when engaging in the negotiating or mediating process. This is where true heartache occurs with parents; when they feel they have had to make a major concession, it is often followed by a sense of anger and resentment toward the other parent, but the parent making the concession is usually just as much to blame as the other parent. It cannot be emphasized enough that parents are not going to get everything they want. They simply are not! But making a major concession is, for example, when a child has to miss a major life event of a family member of one of the parents, or of the parent him- or herself.

The best example I know of avoiding having to make a major concession is a real-life example that happened within my own family. My former husband and father of my son spent every Thanksgiving with my son, and their tradition was to go skiing and snowboarding on Thanksgiving Day, which is a great day to go because very few people are on the slopes on Thanksgiving Day. Even though we did not have anything in writing in regard to our parenting plan (which I don't recommend; most states will not allow separating parents to do this, anyway), we had always agreed that my son and his father would hit the slopes on Thanksgiving Day.

On two occasions during the time my son was growing up and was living primarily in my care, my current husband had a major life event of someone in his family when his parents celebrated their 50th and then their 60th wedding anniversaries. The celebrations, in both instances, occurred out-of-state over Thanksgiving weekend. I acknowledged to my former husband that this was his holiday to spend with the child and that if he wanted our son to stay in Colorado and go snowboarding as they always did, that would happen. But I suggested that we would like to have him be with the family, and kindly, my former husband agreed. "Absolutely, he should be with the rest of the family," he said. "We'll go snowboarding another weekend."

It was not merely because my former husband is kind-hearted that he allowed our son to go with me. It was because for all those years, when it really did not matter if I had Thanksgiving Day with my son or not, I allowed them to have their holiday every year and to establish a tradition. It did not hurt us to celebrate Thanksgiving that following Sunday, after Thanksgiving. We still had a big, festive dinner to celebrate the holiday. In his younger years, my son did not care whether we were celebrating on Thursday or Sunday; he did not know the difference. It did not matter what day of the week it was when we celebrated the holiday. My son simply grew up thinking that Thanksgiving was celebrated on Sunday rather than Thursday.

I could have thrown a fit and insisted on having "my share" of Thanksgiving days. But I gave in when it really did not matter, which made it awfully difficult for my former husband to say no when I asked on one (or two, in this case) occasion to have my son do something different and go with me so that he could be present for a big family event. I did not have to make a major concession. But it was because I had set myself up to not have to make a major concession.

Learning to give in when it does not matter is one of the hardest things separating parents have to learn to do, but it is part of getting what one wants when it really matters. Parents have to decide for themselves what really matters and what doesn't. But too often, *every little thing* matters, because a parent does not want to "give in" to the other parent. He or she does not want to let the other parent "win." Parents have to realize it is more important to "win" when it matters, and the rest of the time, they have to let it go. Too many people are short-sighted when it comes to this, and they cannot see on down the line when things like this are going to happen.

Do not set yourself up to ever have to make a major concession.

Some parents are also afraid that the more they give in, the more the other parent will take. It is contrary to human nature, however, to always take and never give. Immediately after separating, or maybe even for a few years following the separation, parents may still be angry or bitter, and giving is not going to take place. But over time, it will. Anger lessens and bitterness subsides, and most people are not hard-hearted enough to allow another person, especially someone they used to love and care about, to have to make a major concession at a time when a life event happens that they really care about. I have rarely seen this happen, over nearly twenty years of conducting evaluations in family law cases. But one must give in order to get, and this is a simple principle that parents seem to fall short in recognizing, to their own detriment.

Learning to place the needs of the child first should be a parent's other guiding factor. In other words, a parent has to love their child more than they hate the other parent. Just following the separation, this may be difficult for some parents to do. But if they keep their decisions focused on the child or children, rather than on the other parent, the parent will find that it is easier to give in than the parent thought it would be. Knowing that the child will benefit or gain from giving in to the other parent, *not the other parent*, can often make giving in a little easier. Because it really is not about either of the parents in these instances; it is about the child.

I recall an incident in which a father and his eight-year-old daughter came into my office one Monday afternoon, and the daughter would not sit down next to her father once they entered my office. Next thing I knew, when I looked up to ask why she was not sitting down, the little girl had tears streaming down her cheeks. When I asked what was wrong, she told me, while fighting back tears, that her best friend, who was also her cousin on mother's side of the family, had had her birthday party on the Saturday that had just passed, and she had not been not allowed to go. The birthday party, which had been a slumber party, was attended by all of the other girls in their class at school, and all day that Monday (the day they came into my office) she'd had to listen to all of the other girls talk about all of the fun they had had at the party. But this little girl had to miss it because father had said he "Cannot stand to be around those people" (referring to mother's family members). Father could not see through his own anger with mother and her family to recognize the need of his daughter to be present at this event, which was a big deal to a girl this age.

All I could say to this father was, "Well, this is what you get to live with, then." Because that little girl was going to be angry with him for a long time. This father clearly could not set his own needs aside to prioritize the needs of his daughter. Not surprisingly, he did not do very well when it came to the parenting-time recommendations I had to make in that case.

CHAPTER 7

··

Basic Principles of Shared Parenting

T he concept of shared parenting in families that are no longer intact is favored over families in which one parent has "custody" and one parent has "visitation." Many states, as mentioned in Chapter 6, are opting for or at least considering laws that favor shared parenting, in which parents have equal, or nearly equal, parenting time. Except for instances in which there is credible evidence of abuse within the family, shared parenting is rapidly becoming the preferred scenario for families in which parents are no longer together.

To eliminate the perception of children as possessions to be won or lost in a legal battle, many judicial proceedings affecting children now focus on parenting time that eliminates possession of the children by one parent and reinforces the concept of shared parenting as one in which each parent has a clear understanding of their role in shared parenting—a role that includes a healthy relationship between the child and the parent. Although every situation is not ripe for 50/50 parenting time, judges must be given leeway to arrive at a parenting plan that meets the needs of each individual family.

When parents are involved in the break-up of the family unit, a fact that is often overlooked is that the children are often the real losers. They are deprived of the proper guidance that two full-time parents can provide. The cooperative guidance and direction that two parents can provide is essential to the moral and emotional developmental growth of children. Whether together or not, as long as both parents are able to work together to provide for the needs of the child, the child will benefit, as their well-being is prioritized. If parents are unable to work together and thereby simply ignore the problems that children will inevitably have, or blame each other for problems, they place the child at significant risk in regard to their developmental growth and well-being.

Children derive their identity from both of their parents, especially when they are young, and children need the role model of two good parents. Essential to developing their own self-respect, children must maintain respect for both of their parents. When parents put down the other parent, they are putting down the child as well and impeding their healthy growth and development. Although there may be bitterness between parents, it is important not to impose or inflict those feelings upon the child, who will likely internalize them as they are developing their own self-concept and self-worth.

One critical, but simple, concept in ensuring that the interests of the child are served: parents need to focus on the child and not on one another. Unless it somehow affects the child, what the other parent does is really no longer your interest or concern. This is especially true in regard to issues that the court really does not care about, such as having extramarital affairs. Although contrary to the moral compass you are trying to teach your child, unless a child has been directly and personally impacted in a negative way, the court is not going to care what the other parent did. States that are "no-fault" divorce states will most likely not hear issues of infidelity and the like. Therefore, children are subjected to this information during divorce proceedings, and yet the information is useless in determining the parenting-time plan. No useful purpose is served, the child is harmed by learning information that only serves to make them feel worse about him- or herself.

Advice to Divorcing Parents
....

If you find yourself unable to maintain a focus on the child rather than your former partner, seek outside professional help. Many parents carry hurt and resentment, but if your feelings of anger and bitterness are impeding your ability to communicate with the other parent about the best interests of your children, then it may be time to seek out a therapist, pastor, mediator, or other professional to allow you to vent about the hurt and pain without impacting your children in a negative way.

Your ability to encourage the love, affection, and contact between your children and the other parent is the greatest gift you can give your child. As an evaluator for the court, I placed the highest importance on a parent's ability to facilitate and encourage that relationship. Children adjust just fine to the change in the family constellation, as long as they are allowed to love and have substantial contact with both parents.

The following are behaviors to avoid as your children adjust to the change in their family:

1. Refrain from exposing the children to adult issues. They are children and need to be allowed to be children.

2. Do not speak negatively about the other parent in the presence of your children, nor allow other persons to do so. They derive their identity from the two of you; when you put down the other parent, you are putting down the child as well.

3. Do not make your children feel as though they have to choose between the two of

you. Allow them to express their love for both of you freely.

4. Be sensitive in the manner by which you introduce significant others or stepparents into their lives. You might be on down the road from the separation mentally, but your children are not.

5. Do not use your children to relay messages or deliver child support payments to the other parent. The children should not be used as your messengers.

6. Be sensitive to the fact that the children may try to manipulate the situation. If they do not think the two of you will talk, you are creating an environment that is ripe for this type of manipulation.

7. Provide reassurance to your children that both parents still love them and do not try to assume that you know how they feel. Even if you are a child of divorce, every divorce situation is different and individuals respond differently.

There is an art to effective shared parenting, and there are a few rules, or expectations, that come with it. Parents can make their lives much easier if they follow a few basic rules that both parents can grow to expect, knowing that they can count on the other parent to handle things in a certain way. When these rules or expectations are not followed, however, a host of problems can be created by a lack of awareness of what the parent is doing to cause things to become so badly tainted. In principle, the following guidelines can really be summed up by the concept of the Golden Rule—simply treating each other the way you would want to be treated. I like to think of this group as the "advanced rules of coparenting:"

1. Coparents are expected to communicate with each other about decisions or events which affect the children at each parent's house. They are expected to do this prior to discussing them with the children. In other words, refrain from getting the children's hopes up about an event or decision that has not been made yet if it falls on the other parent's time. It will be up to the parent with parenting time to make the decision about whether the children participate in the event or activity or not. By letting the children know about it ahead of time, you're making the parent with parenting time the "bad guy" if

that parent decides that they do not want to allow the children to go.

2. Children staying at one household and communicating with the other parent, regardless of which household they are in at the time, should have an expectation of privacy in talking with the other parent. Emails and text messages should remain private, and telephone calls should not be listened in on, with or without the children having knowledge that it is occurring. Telephone calls should also not be placed on speakerphone, with the other parent listening in. Respect the privacy of the other parent the way you would like the other parent to respect your privacy.

3. Coparents are expected to acknowledge the boundaries between the two households and to respect or uphold those boundaries. While the children are with each parent, that parent is allowed to make decisions within that household without obtaining the permission of the other parent. Such decisions include decisions on chores, allowances, food, clothing, and homework, as well as decisions related to the use of electronics, such as television watching or video games.

Each parent is the boss of his or her own household, and of the children while they are in that household.

4. Effective coparents understand that children will have difficult times in their lives, and the difficult times might have just as well occurred if the parents had stayed together. Communications about the problems need to occur, rather than trying to cover up the problems or conceal them from the other parent. Rather than placing blame and pointing fingers at the other parent for the difficulties that your children have, it is much more effective to work together to try to help the child through these difficult times. This is a time during which your child needs you to work together, not compound their problems by being at odds with one another.

5. Coparents are expected to find a balance between their need to have time with the children, and the children's need to have events and activities of their own, often with other children, separate from their parents. Children will have times when they want to attend the birthday party of another child or participate in some other activity that involves other children. Effective coparents

will be flexible with their parenting time to allow participation in such activities.

These items speak to the ability of parents to place the needs of their children above their own, to understand and value the concept of shared parenting and, most importantly, to recognize the importance to their children of having both parents actively and integrally involved in their lives. Working together with the other parent is the greatest gift you can give your child. Working collaboratively with the other parent is icing on the cake!

CHAPTER 8

∙∙

Myths and Reality Regarding Custody

In this battle known as the family court system, everyone has a war story to tell. Whether it is one of the parents going through a divorce, or one of the professionals working on the case, or a friend or relative of one of the parents, stories seem to grow, and they get bigger every time they are told. Too often, I have people who come into my office and let me know something that someone has told them, and they repeat it as though it is fact. I would like to have a dollar for every time a parent came into my office and said that at a certain age, children can just say where they wish to live, and that is what the court will grant. There are also a lot of stories about what people can and cannot do, and under what circumstances. More times than not, I will have to say the stories are inaccurate, with maybe a sliver of truth.

A few of the myths that seem to float around (and often circle back around a year or two after the last time they were corrected or clarified) just do not seem to ever be placed at rest. Exacerbating the problem is the fact that states may have different statutes that govern the family law court for that particular state. The varying laws from state to state lend themselves to a situation that is confusing, at best, and are often shared among coworkers, for example on a military installation. In an attempt to put them at bay, let me address a few of the more prominent misconceptions.

Depending on the state in which a person lives, children may or may not simply state which parent they wish to live with primarily, and how much time they wish to have with the other parent. Given that the state in which I live does not have such a law, I have never had to deal with the repercussions of such a statute, but I can only imagine the problems with this. The first that comes to mind is, what if the child changes his or her mind, and goes bouncing back and forth between parents? Or what if one child wants one schedule, and another child wants something totally different? This does not support the notion that we attempt to keep children together on the same parenting-time plan.

This brings us to the next story: that the courts attempt to keep siblings together, on the same parenting-time schedule. This one happens to be true, and for good reason. The sibling relationship is the most enduring relationship in one's life (which is not to say it is always the most endearing!). But it is the most enduring, and for this reason the courts tend to place a high priority on siblings staying together, on the same parenting-time schedule. Some parents have suggested to me that one parent take one child and the other parent take another, but rarely, if ever, have I seen the court do this. Typically, siblings are kept together, regardless of the age of the children. Even in situations in which there is a toddler and a teenager, the courts still tend to keep siblings together.

A variation of this is the myth that children are allowed to have no say-so at all, and I have also not found this to be the case. Most children are allowed to have some input to the matter. After all, it is their lives we are talking about. Children are typically allowed input through a custody evaluator or someone of this nature, but they *are* allowed input. Typically speaking, the older the child, the greater the input, but this is not consistently the case either. Maturity is more important than age, and the child's reasons are highly important as well. It becomes obvious when children are trying to get themselves a "better deal," wishing to spend more time with the parent who has the fewest rules or the loosest structure to their household.

There is also the myth that children may be brought to court to testify and tell the judge what they want in the way of parenting time with each of their parents. I cannot think of a more horrible thing to do than to place a child on the witness stand, with both parents looking on, to tell the judge what the child wants the judge to know about their feelings about each of his or her parents. In the rare occasion when a judge allows a child to speak with the judge, it is typically an interview that is conducted in chambers, and no one is present except for the judge and the child. The judge typically removes the black robe to talk with the child, thus appearing more like an ordinary person and less like a judge.

Lastly, there is the myth that parenting time and child support orders are permanent; after all, we call the hearing "Final Orders," don't we? But parenting time and child support orders can always be revisited, although some states have restrictions on how frequently this can happen and how soon following the initial hearing regarding parenting time. In Colorado, for example, there is a two-year restriction, mandating that the parents cannot revisit the issue of parenting time for a period of two years following the last order in regard to parenting time. There are exceptions to any rule, and that is true of this one as well. In cases of endangerment or if one of the parties is going to relocate out of the area in which the parents reside currently, then the parents may have the issue heard earlier than two years after the last time they were in court. This type of restriction, however, at least prevents parents from taking matters back to court every six months, as many people would do exactly that if given the opportunity to do so.

I would be remiss if I failed to mention in any discussion regarding myths about parenting time that it is not a good use of time to dig up all the dirt you can about the other parent and bring it to court to share with the judge. If an issue about a parent has no bearing on the child or children, the court will likely not care a whole lot about the issue, even though it makes for good testimony on the stand. An issue must in some way affect the well-being of the child, or you are merely taking up the court's valuable time by bringing such issues to court.

In conclusion, every judge is different in the things on which they place importance and on matters that they consider worthy of court time. Every judge, however, will tell you that he or she needs "hard facts" more than anything else, if he or she is to consider the information you provide. Sometimes, hard facts can be difficult to find. At the end of the day, the judge will make a decision that he or she feels is in the best interest of your child. Most judges will also tell you that it would have been far better if the parents had been able to decide for themselves what is in the best interest of their children.

CHAPTER 9

....

Final Thoughts

In writing reports for the court in custody cases, I always close with a section entitled, "Final Thoughts," so I thought it was appropriate to do so here. There are a few key thoughts for separating parents to keep in mind as they navigate their way through the family court system. These are what I offer as the "roadmap" as they travel down this journey to being a coparent, which they will be for the rest of their lives.

Whether you are a separating parent yourself, a friend or family member of someone going through separation or divorce, or a professional working with separating parents, these are important thoughts to keep in mind or to share with the parents who are going through this journey in their life, which is often not a journey that they chose for themselves, but one that was chosen for them by someone else. They should be the guiding principles, nonetheless.

Final Thoughts

1. Understand that not everyone working within this system is interested in helping you get through this time with as little conflict as possible. In fact, the opposite is often the case. There are those who stand to benefit or gain from perpetuating the conflict, and it is not your best interest, but *their own*, that they have in mind. Utilize, if necessary, a professional who can help you reach an agreement regarding custody issues, not one who wishes to help you to fight. Beware of the professional who wants to help you "get a better deal," because the better deal they are getting is usually their own!

2. Never place yourself in a position to have to make a major concession. Keep in mind the principle that you will not get everything you want in this situation. Decide for yourself what things you can negotiate on, what things you cannot negotiate on, and what things are open for discussion. Give where you can, so that you do not find yourself in a position of having to make a major concession.

3. Place the needs of your children above your own. Even if you are very angry with the

other parent right now, this is not about you or them, this is about the child or children involved. Respect the fact that the child will always love the other parent. Commit to loving your child more than you hate the other parent. Place their needs above your own. You will never go wrong by doing so.

4. Lastly, remember that at some point in time, there was something you liked about the other parent, and if nothing else, he or she gave you this wonderful child or children, whom you would not have had it not been for the other parent. Keep in mind that your children have a need to be allowed to love both parents. The greatest gift you can give your children is to allow them to love the other parent. And the greatest threat of harm to your children is not whatever it is that you are fighting about, but the conflict itself. Take care of your children, as this is your lasting legacy. Make it one you are proud of, as whatever you teach them today is what they will become tomorrow. Before you give into the temptation to, or allow anyone else to convince you to, make this a contentious process, ask yourself, "Is this really in the best interest of *my* children?"

APPENDIX A

···

My Journey out of Court Evaluations into Speaking and Writing

I cannot say I went willingly into working in the family court arena. In fact, I always depict my entry into this system by saying that I went kicking and screaming into this area of practice.

I was working as a family preservation specialist, which involved in-home counseling services for families involved in dependency and neglect cases within the court system. This provided exposure to court proceedings and involved interfacing with a lot of people who work in the court system, including attorneys.

An attorney asked me one day if I would take a parental responsibilities case (commonly known as a "custody" case, although the state in which I live had discarded the word "custody" many years before). My response was that I never had conducted an evaluation of this nature before, but I was sure that I could. I did not think it would be that difficult to figure out how to determine what was in the best interest of the children embroiled in their parents' divorce. After all, not only was I a trained, well-educated mental health professional, I was also a child of divorce and had been divorced as an adult myself, with a young child at the time. This would certainly give me the personal perspective that I needed to conduct this type of evaluation, on top of my professional qualifications.

I quickly embraced the work as an evaluator and developed a passion for the work I was doing. It did not come immediately, however. In fact, after that first case, I said to myself and others around me, "I will never do that again!" But the need for work won over my initial aversion, and it did not take long for me to develop the passion necessary to not only conduct this type of work, but also to sustain a career in the family court system as a parental responsibilities evaluator (or what is commonly known as a custody evaluator).

I remember the first time that I identified for a child what the child was feeling, when he could not identify it for himself, and I could relate to what he was feeling only because I had been there myself. I recognized the feelings all too well. After both parents in this particular case had told me that something must be wrong in the other parent's household, because when it was time to go to spend time with the other parent, Bobby did not want to go, I sat down with Bobby to discuss what was going on and find out why he did not want to go to the other parent's house.

Bobby assured me that everything was all right in both households, and said that he really did not know why it was that he did not want to go, but he did not deny that this was true. Indeed, he admitted telling each of his parents that he did not want to go, and resisted the back-and-forth existence that had become his way of life. I remember asking Bobby, "Is it that you just don't want to stop what you're doing, perhaps stop playing whatever video game you're playing, pack up your stuff, drive across town, and be in a new environment, with a different set of rules and a different structure to the household?"

To which Bobby replied, "Yes, that's it! Exactly!"

I quickly learned that the very aspect that would lead to my success in this field of practice was my personal experience. My own experience enabled me to relate to what the children I served were going through and the feelings that accompanied that experience.

It also did not take long, however, for me to realize the difficulty in being placed in this position. After all, there is no greater fight in one's life than the fight over the care and control of one's children. And the person placed squarely in the middle of that fight is the person tasked with rendering an opinion to the court about what would be in the children's best interest in terms of time with each of the parents. Certainly there are specific identified items that need to be assessed. But much of the assessment process is subjective, and this is where the problem lies.

Performing custody evaluations for the court is not an exact science. Questioning how one arrived at their conclusions is certainly understandable, and the job of the attorney hired by the parent is to ensure that the evaluator has done his or her job. The part that does not sit well (with this evaluator, anyway), and that seems to thwart the process of determining what is in the best interest of a child, is attacking others, including not only the other parent, but also the professionals who have committed their professional lives to ensuring that competent evaluations are being conducted and that children's lives are managed in a way that is truly in their best interest.

It would be ideal if the child's parents could figure that out, but they are often so far into the middle of the forest to recognize that a tree even exists. In other words, they have often lost their perspective due to a variety of extenuating factors that have nothing to do with the child, such as unfaithfulness during the marriage or financial issues.

Whatever the reason may be, many parents are not, at least at this particular point in time in the parent's life, able to determine what is in the best interest of their children and, therefore, leave it to an expert in this area to determine it for them.

My friend and colleague, Joseph Michelli, PhD, said it best. I met Dr. Michelli in approximately 2003 or 2004, when we were both conducting evaluations for the courts in Colorado Springs, Colorado. I knew that Dr. Michelli had left the field of practice when he authored a bestselling book on, of all things, the Starbucks empire. When I phoned him in November, 2014, to tell him that I thought I wanted to transition into a career as a speaker and writer rather than to continue conducting evaluations for the court, Dr. Michelli's response was, "Yes, I remember the psychological trauma that went along with doing parental responsibilities evaluations for the court."

The *psychological trauma*.

I suddenly felt like that child, Bobby, must have felt when I identified what it was that he was feeling. My friend and colleague had succinctly identified what it was that I was feeling; a need to find a different way to make an impact in this arena without experiencing my own *psychological trauma* by working in this particular area of family court.

In case this sounds dramatic, I believe it is nothing short of that and, although I had not defined it as such, I knew that I was dealing with an area of work that could not, and should not, be taken casually.

I sit with the obituary near me of another friend and colleague of mine, Mark Wilmot, PhD, whom I also met in Colorado Springs many years ago when I started doing this type of work, as a reminder not to take the work too seriously, on a personal level anyway. Attacks on our work, our character, and anything else that can be used to discredit us as evaluators who have made a recommendation that one party does not like, are nothing more than posturing and leveraging that an attorney does to obtain what the client desires in this situation. After all, that is the attorney's job. But some people do not deal well with character assassination that comes with putting oneself in a vulnerable position by offering recommendations about the best interest of a child to a court. I knew something was not right when someone left several boxes of books at the doorstep to my office with nothing on them but my name. The books all had to do with this area of work. It was not until after I had learned the news that Dr. Wilmot had committed suicide that it dawned on me that he might have been the person who left the boxes of books on my doorstep. I hurried to the office and started rummaging through the boxes of books, looking in each book to find any shred of evidence to indicate from where they had come. Sure enough, I found Dr. Wilmot's name scratched on the inside of one of the books. Had Dr. Wilmot fallen victim to the *psychological trauma* that goes along with doing this type of work? I will never know that for sure, but I'd had many discussions with Dr. Wilmot about the attacks that we endure, the criticism that is thrown our way—enough such discussions that I was certain that it had at least come into play to some extent with a man who found that life was just too difficult to endure.

Going back in time seven years, I had endured a very public attack by a fellow mental health professional, leading to a week-long trial for allegations I brought against the individual involved, who we'll call Dr. X. For six years, Dr. X had done things like write letters to previous places where I had been employed and to the school where I obtained both my bachelor's and my master's degrees, Wichita State University. Dr. X would claim that she had been presented with my resume, as though I was applying for work within her practice, and would ask for the business to complete an employment verification form.

The only problem was, Dr. X only included my current name, not my maiden name or my previous married name. The places of employment would respond by stating that no one by that name had ever been employed there. (Of course they would say that, because that was not my name when I was employed there.) Likewise, Wichita State University, from where I had not only obtained two degrees but had also been a cheerleader, responded by saying that no one by that name had ever attended school there. Dr. X then distributed these letters to judges and attorneys in the community, claiming that I was a fraud and did not have the degrees or work experience that I claimed to have. Enduring six years of this was enough, and I hired an attorney, filed a lawsuit for harassment, defamation, and malicious prosecution. I prevailed in that lawsuit, but the expense, both financially and emotionally, was more than I cared to ever endure again. This would certainly put an end to the allegations, however, that I was not qualified to do the work that I do and the other allegations that attorneys and *pro se* parties, parties representing themselves, throw out there. Or would it?

Fast forward seven years, and I found myself caught up in another attack that involved a judge and an unscrupulous attorney. As evaluators in the court system, we must rely on attorneys to inform us of court dates in a case. We are often forgotten when it comes to this task. Attorneys are busy making sure that their clients can be there, as well as ensuring that the hearing date does not conflict with anything else on their calendar. In addition, they have to make sure that they calendar the other dates, such as the pre-trial readiness conference, witness disclosure, and joint trial management due dates, that they often forget to notify the evaluator of the hearing date. In this particular case, the attorneys notified me only days before the hearing, which poses a problem when the evaluator's report is due to the court twenty-one days before the hearing. In addition, the evaluator is typically expected to be there for any contested hearing for which the evaluator has rendered an opinion in regard to parenting time. Being an evaluator in demand, I had already been both subpoenaed and paid to be in another county, several hours away from the district court where I conducted most of my work, to testify at the contested hearing for another case for which I had conducted an evaluation. I could not be in both places at one time, so I prepared a letter to the judge for the local case, explaining my predicament and notifying her that I would not be present at the hearing that was going to be held in her courtroom, also explaining why my report was not completed and submitted by the due date.

There are two ingredients in the family court system that are a recipe for disaster that came into play in my situation: a finicky, demanding judge who does not take well to an expert who says he or she cannot be present at the hearing in her courtroom, and a dishonest attorney. One of the attorneys in this case, the honest one in this matter, informed the judge that I had not been copied on the notice of hearing that had been filed with the court and that she had not informed me of the court date. The other attorney, however, in perhaps an act of self-preservation, informed the judge that she was *sure* her office had notified me of the hearing. This attorney had informed the other attorney and me a few days earlier that she was not really prepared for hearing anyway, and she was planning on requesting a continuance of the hearing date. The honest attorney and I, however, knew that this judge *never* granted continuances of the hearing date. This attorney said that she had sent me an email informing me of the hearing date, all the while shuffling papers around on her table as though she had some kind of evidence of such, while in reality no such email existed. No email ever was produced and never has been to date. Yet I was found by this judge to have failed to perform the work that I was appointed to perform (never mind the fact that I was not notified of the hearing date and had no way of knowing that a report was due; this is when I discovered how contentious and unfair this system really is, or can be).

I do not intend to imply that the whole system operates in this manner, or that there are not judges who genuinely care about the public that they serve, and care about the professionals who work within this system, as there are plenty who do. However, the judge in this case was basing a decision about another professional on *hearsay*—the big "no-no" in family court cases, or any court cases for that matter. And from someone only looking to protect herself, divert blame onto someone else, destroying the reputation of an undeserving colleague, all the while probably sleeping just fine at night, never thinking twice about the damage that was done.

It is my only desire now to heighten people's awareness of the contentiousness that exists within this system, this battleground known as the family court system, and to say there must be a better way to handle divorce and separation than the way we do currently. My tagline and motto have become, "Love your children more than you hate your ex." That is in the best interest of your children.

Warmth and best wishes to you all.

APPENDIX B

Acknowledgments

I would like to express my sincere gratitude to the many people who have supported me in writing this book.

I would like to thank Mark LeBlanc, my mentor and coach, who had a vision for the book and a title for it, even before I did, and who encouraged me by reminding me that this is an important topic and that my thoughts about it needed to be heard and read.

I would like to thank Henry DeVries, my editor and publisher, who believed in me, taught me all that I know (albeit not all that *he* knows!) about writing a book, and who provided patience and encouragement when I needed it most.

And to Mark and Henry, together, for helping me keep the faith.

Thanks to my stepmom, Betty Moser, who listens and cares, and makes me feel supported and uplifted in everything I do.

Thanks to Judge Jann DuBois and Judge Deborah Grohs for always being positive, supportive, and encouraging, even when I was in the midst of turmoil.

Thanks to my NSA (National Speakers Association) family, who have shown me what a truly caring group is all about and restored my faith in people.

Thanks to Joseph Michelli, PhD, for introducing me to the NSA organization, for encouraging me to make this career change, and for believing in me that I could do it.

Thanks specifically to my mastermind group, the Conifer Mastermind Group. The support and encouragement you provide in regard to the work I do has been such a blessing and I am grateful for you all.

Thanks to my husband, Mike, and my son, Aaron Butcher, who always support and encourage me, believe in me, and provide inspiration on a daily basis. Thanks especially to Mike for being my rock and the love of my life, and to Aaron for making me laugh and for believing in me. You guys keep me grounded and are the best cheerleaders a wife and mother could have. Thanks for believing in me the way you do.

APPENDIX C

About the Author

Marlene Bizub, Psy.D. is a speaker, author, and private consultant who has committed her professional life to working with children and families who are going through divorce or separation. Dr. Marlene (a name she uses to be more approachable to the children she serves) began her career as a psychotherapist, then worked nearly twenty years as an evaluator in domestic relations cases for courts in Colorado. She graduated from Wichita State University with a master's degree in gerontology and counseling, attended Colorado School of Professional Psychology, and earned her Doctorate degree in Forensic Psychology from Eisner Institute for Professional Studies.

As a professional speaker and certified divorce coach, Dr. Marlene teaches her negotiation process to divorcing and separating parents and professionals in the family court system so they can guide separating and divorcing parents to avoid contention and negotiate their way to mutual agreement. Dr. Marlene has developed a process for family court professionals to help create a less contentious, adversarial, and stressful environment—and instead create win/win situations—for themselves, their clients, and the children.

Over the years, Dr. Marlene has worked as a family preservation specialist in dependency and neglect cases and has served on various committees for the court. Currently, she serves as a facilitator for the *Children and Families in Transition* class through the 4th Judicial District Court in Colorado Springs. In addition, she is a designated provider of the "For the Kids" Level 2 coparenting workshop through 4th Judicial District Court. A high-energy speaker and compelling storyteller, Dr. Marlene has presented at a number of Continuing Law Education Conferences and Family Law Institute events, and has had articles published in psychotherapy and legal publications.

Dr. Marlene is a member of National Speakers Association as well as a member of the Colorado Chapter of NSA. She has served as the District Director of Women's Ministries for the Wesleyan Church. The devoted mother of a son and stepdaughter, Marlene and her husband own and operate a haunted house for entertainment in Colorado Springs during the Halloween season.

For bulk orders of this book or to inquire about Dr. Marlene as a speaker, please contact her at 719-641-5403 or DrMarlene@MarleneBizub.com.

www.ingramcontent.com/pod-product-compliance
Lightning Source LLC
Chambersburg PA
CBHW031949190326
41519CB00007B/732